I AM THAT I AM

Unlocking God's Promises:

Activate His Power In Your Life.

BY: ARIE J. BROOKS

Copyright © 2025 by Seazons Collections Publishing House.

Copyright © 2025 by Scirocca Publication.

Copyright © 2025 by Arie J. Brooks.

All rights reserved. No part of this book may be reproduced or used in any manner without written permission of the copyright owner.

TABLE OF CONTENTS

Dedication	1
Introduction	2
I Am Who You Say I Am	5
I Speak with the Tongue of the Learned and the Wise	8
I Shall Live and Not Die	11
I Am Walking in God's Purpose for My Life	14
I Have the Mind of Christ	17
I Am Free from Condemnation	20
I Am Walking in Divine Favor	23
I Am a Child of God	26
I Am a Financial Tycoon for God's Kingdom	29
I Am the Head and Not the Tail	32
I Am Healed	35

I Am Redeemed	39
I Can Do All Things Through Christ	42
I Declare That No Weapon Formed Against Me Shall Prosper	45
I Please God in Everything That I Do	48
I Am Holy and Blameless in the Sight of the Lord	51
I Declare That I Am a Money Magnet —Money Finds Me	54
I Declare That All My Needs Are Met, I'm Out of Debt, and I Have Plenty More to Put in Store	57
Lord, Remove Anything in Me That Displeases You	60
I Decree Supernatural Recall Over My Mind	63
Lord, Keep My Mind in Perfect Peace	66
Let the Words of My Mouth and the Meditation of My Heart Be Acceptable to You	69
I Take Captive Every Thought to Make It Obedient to Christ	72
Lord, Purify My Heart	75

I Declare and Decree That My Latter Will Be Greater Than My Former	78
I Walk in Love and Forgiveness	81
My Weapons of Warfare Are Not Carnal, but Mighty Through God	85
Lord, Above All Else, Help Me to Love Like You and Carry Out Your Will	88
Lord, Open the Eyes of My Understanding	92
I Am a Generational Curse Breaker	95
I Am a Yoke Destroyer	99
I Am an Atmosphere Changer	101
I Am a Believer of Authority	103
Sinner's Prayer	105

DEDICATION

This book is dedicated to Believers of Authority Ministries Inc., where Apostle Dr. John H. Chambers III serves as the Founder and Senior Pastor.

God placed me in this ministry, a place where I have been spiritually fed and strengthened in the Word of God. Under the leadership and teaching of my pastor, I have learned the power of confession and the authority of spoken words. His divine assignment in the earth realm is to teach the world how to "talk," aligning our words with the will of God to bring forth supernatural manifestations.

I am forever grateful for this ministry, for the Word that has taken root in my life, and for the anointed teaching that has transformed my understanding of faith, authority, and confession.

With gratitude and honor,
Arie Joy

~ ~

INTRODUCTION

The biblical meaning of the number 33 represents God's promises. In Scripture, there are 7,487 documented promises from God. I have taken the liberty of turning 33 of these promises into daily confessions for your life. Jesus lived for 33 years and represents the manifestation of the Promise of Salvation.

The power of confession is real. Proverbs 18:21 declares, "Death and life are in the power of the tongue, and those who love it shall eat the fruit thereof." Your words shape your life and the world around you. God's Word carries power, and confession brings possession. You should always speak what you desire because, in time, you will have what you say. Your words are seeds—when spoken in faith, they produce fruit.

These daily confessions are designed to be declared over your life and the lives of your loved ones. As you speak them, expect supernatural change and the manifestation of God's glory.

God created man to rule and have dominion on the earth (Genesis 1:26). Through His Word, He has given us authority—it is our responsibility to operate in it. When we speak life, align our words with God's truth, and walk in faith, we activate His promises in our lives.

Speak boldly. Confess daily. Walk in your God-given authority.

I AM THAT, I AM

I AM THAT I AM

CONFESSION....

1 PETER 2:9-10

But ye are a chosen generation, a royal priesthood, an holy nation, a peculiar people; that ye should shew forth the praises of him who hath called you out of darkness into his marvelous light; Which in time past were not a people, but are now the people of God: which had not obtained mercy, but now have obtained mercy.

I AM WHO YOU SAY I AM

"But you are a chosen generation, a royal priesthood, a holy nation, His own special people, that you may proclaim the praises of Him who called you out of darkness into His marvelous light."

—1 Peter 2:9

Remind God that He called and chose you for such a time as this. You are who you are because He created you with purpose and destiny.

Put the Lord in remembrance of His Word, declaring that you are who He has predestined you to be from the foundation of the world. When you speak this truth, believe it with unwavering Faith.

I AM THAT I AM

CONFESSION....

Isaiah 50:4-5

The Lord God hath given me the tongue of the learned, that I should know how to speak a word in season to him that is weary: he wakeneth morning by morning, he wakeneth mine ear to hear as the learned. The Lord God hath opened mine ear, and I was not rebellious, neither turned away back.

I Speak with the Tongue of the Learned and the Wise

"The Lord God has given me the tongue of the learned, that I should know how to speak a word in season to him who is weary."

—**Isaiah 50:4**

Life's challenges will test your faith and tempt you to waver in your communication with God. However, no matter the situation, you must choose to speak life, regardless of what it looks like.

Speaking life is like learning to ride a bike—it requires practice. If you never start, you'll never grow in it. Work at speaking with wisdom, clarity, and understanding. The more you declare this over yourself, the more it becomes your portion.

Train yourself daily to speak God's truth, and in time, speaking life will become your natural response.

I AM THAT I AM

CONFESSION....

Psalm 118:17-18

I shall not die, but live, and declare the works of the Lord. The Lord hath chastened me sore: but he hath not given me over unto death.

I Shall Live and Not Die

"I shall not die, but live, and declare the works of the Lord."

—Psalm 118:17

The Bible tells us that the enemy comes to steal, kill, and destroy, but Jesus came that we may have life and have it more abundantly.

—John 10:10

Sickness and disease are not from God. Whatever lie the enemy has told you about your health, don't believe it. Doubt the doubt—never doubt God's Word. If you are facing adversity and challenges with your health, make this your daily declaration. Stand on His promise and declare with faith: I shall live and not die, in Jesus' name!

I AM THAT I AM

CONFESSION....

JEREMIAH 29:11-12

For I know the thoughts that I think toward you, saith the Lord, thoughts of peace, and not of evil, to give you an expected end. Then shall ye call upon me, and ye shall go and pray unto me, and I will hearken unto you.

I Am Walking in God's Purpose for My Life

"For I know the plans I have for you," declares the Lord, "plans to prosper you and not to harm you, plans to give you hope and a future."

—Jeremiah 29:11

At some point in life, we all experience uncertainty about God's purpose for us. This is why it's important to declare His promises daily.

The Bible also says, "Faith without works is dead."

—James 2:26

If you are unsure of what God has called you to do, seek Him for instruction. Spend time in prayer, fasting, and studying His Word.

God is also a God of order. Submit to your spiritual covering and leadership, allowing them to help guide you in your assignment. Write the vision; make it plain (Habakkuk 2:2), and trust that as you seek Him, He will reveal His divine purpose for your life.

I AM THAT I AM

CONFESSION....

1 Corinthians 2:16

For who hath known the mind of the Lord, that he may instruct him? but we have the mind of Christ.

I Have the Mind of Christ

"For who has known the mind of the Lord that he may instruct Him? But we have the mind of Christ."

—1 Corinthians 2:16

Research shows that the average person has approximately 60,000 thoughts per day. Even more concerning is that 75% of these thoughts are negative, and 95% are repetitive.

The devil operates by presenting thoughts, ideas, and suggestions. Often, we unknowingly accept negative thoughts, failing to recognize that they did not originate from us. As believers, we have the mind of Christ!

The next time a thought arises that does not align with God's Word or His purpose for your life, cast it down in Jesus' name!

—2 Corinthians 10:5

I AM THAT I AM

Confession....

Romans 8:1

There is therefore now no condemnation to them which are in Christ Jesus, who walk not after the flesh, but after the Spirit. For the law of the Spirit of life in Christ Jesus hath made me free from the law of sin and death.

I Am Free from Condemnation

"There is therefore now no condemnation for those who are in Christ Jesus."

—Romans 8:1

We have all sinned and fallen short of the glory of God (Romans 3:23), yet God does not condemn us. Condemnation is not from God but from the devil.

The Spirit of God brings conviction, not condemnation. Conviction leads us to repentance, pressing upon our hearts to change our behavior, attitude, and perspective. It does not beat us down but lifts us up into God's grace.

It's okay to fall down—just don't stay down. If you choose to remain down, condemnation will keep you there. But if you repent and choose to walk in God's grace, conviction will guide you to transformation. Dust yourself off, walk in the victory of Christ, and move forward in Faith!

I AM THAT I AM

CONFESSION....

Psalm 5:12

For thou, Lord, wilt bless the righteous; with favour wilt thou compass him as with a shield.

I Am Walking in Divine Favor

"For You, O Lord, will bless the righteous; with favor You will surround him as with a shield."

—Psalm 5:12

Divine favor is a gift from God. Favor is defined as God using someone else's power, influence, and ability on your behalf to accomplish what you cannot do alone. I thank God daily for the gift of His favor. When you learn to appreciate this gift, you become grateful for even the small things.

A parking spot opening up right in front of your destination, an unexpected opportunity, or a door opening that you didn't even knock on—these are all manifestations of God's favor. Ask God for His favor today and every day, and watch Him move on your behalf!

I AM THAT I AM

Confession....

John 1:12-13

But as many as received him, to them gave he power to become the sons of God, even to them that believe on his name: Which were born, not of blood, nor of the will of the flesh, nor of the will of man, but of God.

I Am a Child of God

"Yet to all who did receive Him, to those who believed in His name, He gave the right to become children of God."

—John 1:12

Everyone is a creation of God, but not everyone is God's child. Jesus told Nicodemus, "Except a man be born again, he cannot see the kingdom of God." (John 3:3)

If you have accepted Jesus Christ as your Lord and Savior, then you are not only God's creation—you are His child. Walk in the confidence of your identity in Christ, knowing that you belong to Him.

I AM THAT I AM

CONFESSION....

Deuteronomy 8:18-19

But thou shalt remember the Lord thy God: for it is he that giveth thee power to get wealth, that he may establish his covenant which he sware unto thy fathers, as it is this day. And it shall be, if thou do at all forget the Lord thy God, and walk after other gods, and serve them, and worship them, I testify against you this day that ye shall surely perish.

I Am a Financial Tycoon for God's Kingdom

"But remember the Lord your God, for it is He who gives you the ability to produce wealth."

—Deuteronomy 8:18

I declare that my family and I are financial tycoons for God's Kingdom. God created us to have dominion, authority, and power over every creeping thing on the earth. Money doesn't rule us—we rule money. It is a tool that God has given us to help fund His Kingdom.

Many people desire to be millionaires and billionaires for selfish gain, but what does it profit a man to gain the whole world and lose his soul? (Mark 8:36). True wealth is Kingdom wealth. There are many ways to make money, but there is only one way to keep it—by serving God, not money.

I declare that I am a financial tycoon for the Lord's business. I receive the increase, and I steward it for His glory!

I AM THAT I AM

CONFESSION....

Deuteronomy 28:13-14

And the Lord shall make thee the head, and not the tail; and thou shalt be above only, and thou shalt not be beneath; if that thou hearken unto the commandments of the Lord thy God, which I command thee this day, to observe and to do them: And thou shalt not go aside from any of the words which I command thee this day, to the right hand, or to the left, to go after other gods to serve them.

I Am the Head and Not the Tail

"The Lord will make you the head and not the tail; you shall be above only, and not beneath."

—Deuteronomy 28:13

When we come into the realization of who we are, our days of settling for less than we deserve will be over. Our value is far greater than what the enemy wants us to believe. God didn't just give us power—He gave us power and authority because we are created in His image.

Therefore, I boldly declare that I am the head and not the tail, above and not beneath, the lender and not the borrower.

In Jesus' name, decree it, believe it, and receive it!

I AM THAT I AM

CONFESSION....

Isaiah 53:5-6

But he was wounded for our transgressions, he was bruised for our iniquities: the chastisement of our peace was upon him; and with his stripes we are healed. All we like sheep have gone astray; we have turned every one to his own way; and the Lord hath laid on him the iniquity of us all.

I Am Healed

"By His stripes we are healed."

—Isaiah 53:5

My daily confession is this: By the stripes of Jesus Christ, I am healed!

In February 2025, I went for a routine check-up with my primary care physician. I felt completely normal with no symptoms. That same day, I had blood work done, and the next day, my results were in. At my follow-up visit, my doctor told me I was anemic—so severely iron-deficient that I was just one level away from needing a blood transfusion. However, there was still time to make it right. I was immediately scheduled to begin iron treatments with CTU.

This is a testimony of God's mercy, love, and the power of His Word. Every day, I make a conscious decision to speak life, whether the adversity I face is seen or unseen. God's Word is the greatest preventive measure known to man. Because His Spirit moves through me, my declarations of faith disrupted the enemy's plans against me and He sent them back to the sender!

Speaking life and standing on God's Word brings supernatural results. As we declare His promises, Jesus intercedes, and our Heavenly Father moves on our behalf. Today, I am anemia-free because whom the Son sets free is free indeed! Glory be to God!

I AM THAT I AM

CONFESSION....

Ephesians 1:7-9

In whom we have redemption through his blood, the forgiveness of sins, according to the riches of his grace; Wherein he hath abounded toward us in all wisdom and prudence; Having made known unto us the mystery of his will, according to his good pleasure which he hath purposed in himself:

I Am Redeemed

"In Him we have redemption through His blood, the forgiveness of sins, according to the riches of His grace."

—Ephesians 1:7

I haven't always walked the right path—I have a past. But God not only forgave me, delivered me, and set me free; He redeemed me! Through Jesus Christ, my Lord and Savior, I am washed clean by His blood.

Not everyone can say they have been redeemed, but as children of God, we have the right to claim it. What a powerful blessing it is to be redeemed! Because of Jesus, I have access to His blood, His name, and His Word.

I am redeemed, and I walk in that truth daily!

I AM THAT I AM

CONFESSION....

Philippians 4:13-14

I can do all things through Christ which strengtheneth me. Notwithstanding ye have well done, that ye did communicate with my affliction.

I Can Do All Things Through Christ

"I can do all things through Christ who strengthens me."

—Philippians 4:13

Adversity will come, but it doesn't define us. Greater is He who is in us than he who is in the world (1 John 4:4). My confession is that I can do all things through Christ who strengthens me—and so can you!

The next time you face opposition, whether from a person, place, or situation, remind yourself that God cannot and will not mismanage your life. His strength is made perfect in your weakness, and through Him, you can do all things!

I AM THAT I AM

CONFESSION....

Isaiah 54:17

No weapon that is formed against thee shall prosper; and every tongue that shall rise against thee in judgment thou shalt condemn. This is the heritage of the servants of the Lord, and their righteousness is of me, saith the Lord.

I Declare That No Weapon Formed Against Me Shall Prosper

"No weapon formed against you shall prosper, and every tongue which rises against you in judgment you shall condemn."

—Isaiah 54:17

God never said the weapons wouldn't form; He said they wouldn't prosper. The enemy's only mission is to make those weapons succeed, but they won't—not on God's watch! The Lord has already provided a way of escape, even in the face of temptation (1 Corinthians 10:13).

When you boldly declare that no weapon formed against you shall prosper, you are proclaiming that every plot, plan, and assignment of the enemy is nullified and canceled in the spirit realm.

Rest in the promise that even when the weapons form, no harm shall come near your dwelling (Psalm 91:10). That is the Word of the Living God.

I AM THAT I AM

Confession....

1 Corinthians 10:31-33

Whether therefore ye eat, or drink, or whatsoever ye do, do all to the glory of God. Give none offence, neither to the Jews, nor to the Gentiles, nor to the church of God: Even as I please all men in all things, not seeking mine own profit, but the profit of many, that they may be saved.

I Please God in Everything That I Do

"So whether you eat or drink or whatever you do, do it all for the glory of God."

—1 Corinthians 10:31

Everything you do should be done as if it is being done for the Lord. Your everyday actions matter to God. When you set your heart on pleasing Him in all that you do, this confession will shape your life.

If your greatest desire is to one day hear, "Well done, my good and faithful servant" (Matthew 25:23), then make this a daily declaration. And don't just say it with your mouth—believe it in your heart, because God looks at the heart (1 Samuel 16:7).

I AM THAT I AM

Confession....

Ephesians 1:4-6

According as he hath chosen us in him before the foundation of the world, that we should be holy and without blame before him in love: Having predestinated us unto the adoption of children by Jesus Christ to himself, according to the good pleasure of his will, To the praise of the glory of his grace, wherein he hath made us accepted in the beloved.

I AM HOLY AND BLAMELESS IN THE SIGHT OF THE LORD

"For He chose us in Him before the creation of the world to be holy and blameless in His sight."

—Ephesians 1:4

The enemy loves to send people to remind you of your past—who you were and where you came from. But it's not about who you were; it's about who you are now!

You are a new creation in Christ (2 Corinthians 5:17), made brand new by His grace. When the enemy tries to bring up your past, remind him of your future! You are holy and blameless in the sight of the Lord, chosen before the foundation of the world!

I AM THAT I AM

CONFESSION....

Deuteronomy 8:18-19

But thou shalt remember the Lord thy God: for it is he that giveth thee power to get wealth, that he may establish his covenant which he sware unto thy fathers, as it is this day. And it shall be, if thou do at all forget the Lord thy God, and walk after other gods, and serve them, and worship them, I testify against you this day that ye shall surely perish.

I Declare That I Am a Money Magnet—Money Finds Me

"But remember the Lord your God, for it is He who gives you the ability to produce wealth."

—Deuteronomy 8:18

The enemy often attacks finances first (see Job 1:1-11) because he knows that lack can discourage believers. Job was blessed, and his substance increased in the land, yet Satan targeted his wealth. Likewise, when you say yes to God, financial attacks may come—but don't be discouraged.

God will also test your financial stewardship to build character and integrity within you. However, when you remain faithful despite the season you're in, money will find you. Money is a tool, and because God has given us power and authority, we have the ability to command financial increase to locate us.

Declare today that you are a money magnet for the Kingdom of God—and provision, increase, and overflow will always be your portion, in Jesus' name!

I AM THAT I AM

Confession....

Philippians 4:19

But my God shall supply all your need according to his riches in glory by Christ Jesus. Now unto God and our Father be glory for ever and ever. Amen.

I Declare That All My Needs Are Met, I'm Out of Debt, and I Have Plenty More to Put in Store

"And my God shall supply all your need according to His riches in glory by Christ Jesus."

—Philippians 4:19

God is the ultimate source of provision—the greatest distribution center in existence. The earth belongs to Him, and He provides for His people abundantly. As a faithful tither and Kingdom investor, I can testify that God rewards those who seek Him first (Matthew 6:33).

Debt is not my portion! When I surrendered my life to Jesus, I also surrendered financial lack, high interest rates, car loans, and payday loans. Because I serve a limitless God, I live in His abundance. I walk in financial freedom, and my storehouses are overflowing!

I AM THAT I AM

Confession....

Psalm 139:23

Search me, O God, and know my heart: try me, and know my thoughts: And see if there be any wicked way in me, and lead me in the way everlasting.

Lord, Remove Anything in Me That Displeases You

"Search me, O God, and know my heart; test me and know my anxious thoughts."

—Psalm 139:23

We were all born in sin and shaped in iniquity (Psalm 51:5). Before coming to Christ, we lived by the world's standards, and even after salvation, we must continually allow the Holy Spirit to purify us.

The flesh is stubborn, but with God, transformation is possible. The more we love Him, the more we desire to please Him. Ask God daily to search your heart and remove anything that displeases Him—so that you may reflect His holiness in all that you do.

Make this confession personal: Lord, purge me, refine me, and shape me into the vessel You created me to be!

I AM THAT I AM

CONFESSION....

John 14:26

But the Comforter, which is the Holy Ghost, whom the Father will send in my name, he shall teach you all things, and bring all things to your remembrance, whatsoever I have said unto you.

I Decree Supernatural Recall Over My Mind

"But the Helper, the Holy Spirit… will teach you all things and bring to your remembrance all things that I said to you."

—John 14:26

Growing up, I often heard people say, "I don't know if I'm coming or going!" or "I just can't remember!" Words like these shape our reality, and many unknowingly speak defeat over their minds.

But when I became a believer, I learned that my words have power (Proverbs 18:21). Now, I declare:

- I have supernatural recall and a sharp mind.
- My memory is blessed, and I retain every good thing.
- I have the mind of Christ, and confusion has no place in me!

Declare this over your life—speak blessings over your mind, and watch your recall increase!

I AM THAT I AM

Confession....

Isaiah 26:3-5

Thou wilt keep him in perfect peace, whose mind is stayed on thee: because he trusteth in thee. Trust ye in the Lord for ever: for in the Lord Jehovah is everlasting strength: For he bringeth down them that dwell on high; the lofty city, he layeth it low; he layeth it low, even to the ground; he bringeth it even to the dust.

LORD, KEEP MY MIND IN PERFECT PEACE

"You will keep in perfect peace those whose minds are steadfast, because they trust in You."

—Isaiah 26:3

True peace is only found in trusting God. If you're anxious, restless, or worried, ask yourself: Am I truly trusting the Lord?

God's timing is perfect, even when it doesn't align with our expectations. James 1:6 reminds us that wavering faith makes us unstable, but when we fully trust in God, our minds remain at peace.

Today, I choose peace over panic, faith over fear, and trust over doubt. I declare that my mind is kept in perfect peace!

I AM THAT I AM

CONFESSION....

PSALM 19:14

Let the words of my mouth, and the meditation of my heart, be acceptable in thy sight, O Lord, my strength, and my redeemer.

Let the Words of My Mouth and the Meditation of My Heart Be Acceptable to You

"Let the words of my mouth and the meditation of my heart be acceptable in Your sight, O Lord."

—**Psalm 19:14**

Before I was saved by grace, I thought I had it all together—didn't we all? But even as a believer, I have fallen short. None of us is perfect, but we must be intentional about speaking words that please God.

When you desire to honor God with your words, you will be:

- Slow to speak (James 1:19)
- Quick to listen
- Slow to anger

Ask God to refine your speech so that every word you speak reflects His truth and grace!

I AM THAT I AM

Confession....

Colossians 3:2-4

Set your affection on things above, not on things on the earth. For ye are dead, and your life is hid with Christ in God. When Christ, who is our life, shall appear, then shall ye also appear with him in glory.

I Take Captive Every Thought to Make It Obedient to Christ

"Set your minds on things above, not on earthly things."

—**Colossians 3:2**

Not all thoughts that enter your mind are your own, which is why you must take them captive when they try to set themselves against the knowledge of Christ. Thoughts are loud in the heavenly realm, but we must cast down every imagination and high thought that does not align with God's truth.

As 2 Corinthians 10:5 states, though our thoughts may be loud in the heavens, nothing happens until we speak them aloud. There is power in speaking.

Do not allow the enemy to keep your mouth shut, nor let him deceive you into speaking contrary to God's Word. Words are life, and you shall speak life according to the knowledge you have of God's Word. In Jesus' name!

I AM THAT I AM

CONFESSION....

Psalm 51:10-12

Create in me a clean heart, O God; and renew a right spirit within me. Cast me not away from thy presence; and take not thy holy spirit from me. Restore unto me the joy of thy salvation; and uphold me with thy free spirit.

Lord, Purify My Heart

"Create in me a clean heart, O God, and renew a right spirit within me."

—**Psalm 51:10**

Most of us have experienced hardships at some point in our lives—whether in childhood, our teenage years, or adulthood. The cares of this world and the challenges we face can taint our hearts. If we are not careful, we may fall into hatred, unforgiveness, lust, greed, pride, and every other thing that is not like God.

That is why we must ask the Lord to purify our hearts. We need Him to create clean hearts within us and renew a right spirit so that, despite what we have been through, we can still think, talk, and act like God. We are His children, made in His image. We cannot allow our past to affect our future. We must make a conscious decision to be like God and to keep our hearts pure before Him!

I AM THAT I AM

CONFESSION....

HAGGAI 2:9

The glory of this latter house shall be greater than of the former, saith the Lord of hosts: and in this place will I give peace, saith the Lord of hosts.

I Declare and Decree That My Latter Will Be Greater Than My Former

"The glory of this present house will be greater than the glory of the former house," says the Lord Almighty. "And in this place, I will grant peace."

—Haggai 2:9

My confession is that my past life does not compare to the life God has in store for me—the life I am living today. I refuse to allow my past to hinder me or keep me bound from receiving the goodness of the Lord and all that He has for me.

God's Word declares that we go from glory to glory, and I choose to take Him at His Word. My past does not compare to my future—my life is just beginning. If you thought you were doing well without God, surrender to Him and watch how you grow by leaps and bounds, both spiritually and in the marketplace.

Your life doesn't end when you take up your cross and follow God—it truly begins!

I AM THAT I AM

CONFESSION....

Ephesians 1:18-23

The eyes of your understanding being enlightened; that ye may know what is the hope of his calling, and what the riches of the glory of his inheritance in the saints, And what is the exceeding greatness of his power to usward who believe, according to the working of his mighty power, Which he wrought in Christ, when he raised him from the dead, and set him at his own right hand in the heavenly places, Far above all principality, and power, and might, and dominion, and every name that is named, not only in this world, but also in that which is to come: And hath put all things under his feet, and gave him to be the head over all things to the church, Which is his body, the fulness of him that filleth all in all.

I Walk in Love and Forgiveness

"And walk in love, as Christ also hath loved us and hath given Himself for us an offering and a sacrifice to God for a sweet-smelling savor."

—Ephesians 5:2

Hurt people hurt people—including God's people. Refusing to walk in love and forgiveness is a refusal to please God. It also grants the enemy access to your life.

Like you, I have been hurt, mistreated, and taken for granted, but I choose to walk in love daily. When I stand before God, what people did to me won't matter. What will matter is how I responded.

The Bible tells us to take no offense (2 Corinthians 6:3). Yet, another scripture says, "Woe to the person through whom the offense comes." (Matthew 18:7)

Do not worry about what people have done to you—leave that to the Lord. You are only responsible for your response.

Forgive daily. Just as you ask God for forgiveness each

day, extend that same mercy to those who have wronged you. "Love covers a multitude of sins." (1 Peter 4:8) Love only thinks the best!

I AM THAT I AM

CONFESSION....

Galatians 3:13-14

Christ hath redeemed us from the curse of the law, being made a curse for us: for it is written, Cursed is every one that hangeth on a tree: That the blessing of Abraham might come on the Gentiles through Jesus Christ; that we might receive the promise of the Spirit through faith.

My Weapons of Warfare Are Not Carnal, but Mighty Through God

"For the weapons of our warfare are not carnal but mighty in God for pulling down strongholds."

—2 Corinthians 10:4

We must remind ourselves not to be carnally minded. Because we live in a physical body, we naturally feel emotions. However, we have a responsibility to respond as God would.

Ephesians 6:12 reminds us that "we wrestle not against flesh and blood, but against principalities, powers, rulers of darkness, and spiritual wickedness in high places."

Our battle is not against people—it is against the spirits influencing them. The enemy often uses those closest to us to create turmoil and division. But God is not the author of confusion. Where there is God, there is unity and divine peace!

I AM THAT I AM

CONFESSION....

Isaiah 10:27

And it shall come to pass in that day, that his burden shall be taken away from off thy shoulder, and his yoke from off thy neck, and the yoke shall be destroyed because of the anointing.

LORD, ABOVE ALL ELSE, HELP ME TO LOVE LIKE YOU AND CARRY OUT YOUR WILL

"Love the Lord your God with all your heart and with all your soul and with all your strength."

—Deuteronomy 6:5

The more we abide in God as His sons and daughters, the more our desire grows to please Him and fulfill His will and purpose for our lives. When you reflect on everything you've been through—the challenges, the trials, and the victories—you gain a deeper awareness of and love for God. Even if the Lord did nothing else for me, He has already given me a second chance through Jesus Christ. He demonstrated His love at the highest level when He gave His only begotten Son for me (John 3:16).

I have one son, and I couldn't fathom giving him up for a world that doesn't love me. Could you? Yet, that's the kind of God we serve—faithful to us even when we are unfaithful to Him. We can't earn the love of God; He is love, and He loves all His children.

In our weaknesses, we must ask the Lord to help us carry out His will for our lives and to love His people unconditionally. Often, people carry deep wounds and struggles, and they need to experience the love of God to be set free. However, if you don't have heaven inside of you, you are not qualified to love the hell out of someone else!

I AM THAT I AM

Confession....

Romans 12:2

And be not conformed to this world: but be ye transformed by the renewing of your mind, that ye may prove what is that good, and acceptable, and perfect, will of God.

LORD, OPEN THE EYES OF MY UNDERSTANDING

"The eyes of your understanding being enlightened; that you may know what is the hope of His calling, and what the riches of the glory of His inheritance in the saints."

—Ephesians 1:18

The Bible reminds us that we have not because we ask not. When you ask God to open your eyes, He will. He will begin to reveal things to you that you could never understand on your own. We need God's help to comprehend His Word, His will, and His ways. Too often, we rely on our own understanding instead of seeking His perspective. However, trying to make sense of God's process with human reasoning will only lead to frustration.

When God opens the eyes of your understanding, you become spiritually awake and enlightened. Confessing Ephesians 1:18 daily will transform your life, your perception, and your point of view. We must seek God's perspective in all things because until we receive His understanding, every false way will seem right!

I AM THAT I AM

CONFESSION....

John 3:1-5

There was a man of the Pharisees, named Nicodemus, a ruler of the Jews: The same came to Jesus by night, and said unto him, Rabbi, we know that thou art a teacher come from God: for no man can do these miracles that thou doest, except God be with him. Jesus answered and said unto him, Verily, verily, I say unto thee, Except a man be born again, he cannot see the kingdom of God. Nicodemus saith unto him, How can a man be born when he is old? can he enter the second time into his mother's womb, and be born? Jesus answered, Verily, verily, I say unto thee, Except a man be born of water and of the Spirit, he cannot enter into the kingdom of God.

I AM A GENERATIONAL CURSE BREAKER

I break curses; I am a generational curse breaker! If we want to see our children and future generations serve God, we must break the generational curses now. The enemy has an algorithm for our lives, but we must be determined to disrupt that cycle and establish a new pattern of righteousness. If we fail to overcome the strongholds in our own lives, we will pass them down for our children to battle.

The Bible instructs us to "train up a child in the way he should go, and when he is old, he will not depart from it" (Proverbs 22:6). A well-known preacher once said, "This walk with God is not just another lesson for your journal but life for your journey." Everything we learn in our walk with God should be passed down to the next generation so they can go into the world, establish spiritual boundaries, and break the curses the enemy has set.

When you come into the full knowledge of who God is and who He created you to be, along with the generations after you, you will walk in power, authority, and dominion—possessing the land as God has decreed!

....

I AM THAT I AM

Confession....

I Am a Yoke Destroyer

I carry a yoke-destroying anointing. Scripture declares that it is the anointing of God upon our lives that destroys the works of the enemy. The enemy wants us to carry burdens—ones meant to keep us bound so that future generations inherit the same struggles. But we must speak life and stand in confidence, knowing that the anointing upon us has the power to break every yoke of bondage (Isaiah 10:27).

The next time a situation arises, speak life. Declare and decree God's Word over it—take authority and break the yoke with the anointing God has placed within you. When you feel weary and burdened, remember this: the Lord's yoke is easy, and His burden is light. You are a yoke destroyer, and the Lord your God will give you rest in your time of need (Matthew 11:28-30).

I AM THAT I AM

Confession....

I Am an Atmosphere Changer

True change starts from within. We often pray for change, but that change must first begin in us. When you become changed, that transformation positively affects everyone around you and those you are connected to. To truly be an atmosphere changer, you must first be transformed by the renewing of your mind (Romans 12:2).

When you think like God and speak like God, you can then operate like God on the earth. Atmosphere changers shift situations, cities, counties, countries, and nations. The twelve disciples whom Jesus chose were atmosphere changers who transformed the world. If you are willing to be renewed in your mind, God will be seen in your life!

I AM THAT I AM

CONFESSION....

I Am a Believer of Authority

There is an authority that many believers do not fully recognize that we have. Before Jesus returns, there will be a company of believers who will rise up and walk boldly in the authority given to them. We will do the work that God has assigned to us.

Some people believe the devil has authority, but he does not. He has power—but even that power is limited. If God had not allowed him to be the prince of the air, he would have no power at all.

As believers, we receive authority when we are born again. We are made new creatures in Christ and inherit the name of the Lord Jesus Christ, which we can use in prayer and spiritual warfare against the enemy.

I take authority in the spirit realm when I war against the kingdom of darkness. I use my authority when praying over my home, my child, my spouse, and my family. As a believer of authority, God has given me the ability, the right, and the power to rule over the enemy and his kingdom. I will use my authority for the glory of God!

I AM THAT I AM

CONFESSION....

Sinner's Prayer

"Jesus saith unto him, I am the way, the truth, and the life: no man cometh unto the Father, but by me."

The promises of God that we have declared over our lives are of no effect to us if we are not born-again children of God. The only way to become a child of God is to accept Jesus Christ as your Lord and Savior. Everyone is God's creation, but not everyone is His child.

This next confession is the greatest confession of all time—the most important one you will ever make. If you have never accepted Jesus as your Savior, or if you have backslidden and gotten off track, confess the sinner's prayer with me:

Heavenly Father,

Thank You for sending Your Son, Jesus Christ, to die for my sins. Forgive me for all my sins. I accept Jesus Christ as my Lord and Savior. Teach me to live in a way that pleases You. Thank You for Your forgiveness and for filling me with Your Holy Spirit.

In Jesus' name, I pray.

Amen!

Made in the USA
Columbia, SC
29 March 2025